Birds

Birds

By Jaromír Zpěvák

SUNBURST BOOKS

Text by Jaromír Zpěvák
Translated by Alena Linhartová
Illustrations by Jaromír Zpěvák
Graphic design by Ivan Zpěvák

Designed and produced by Aventinum
English language edition first published in 1994
by Sunburst Books, Deacon House,
65 Old Church Street, London SW3 5BS

ISBN 1 85778 024 8
Printed in Slovakia
1/25/01/51-01

CONTENTS

INTRODUCTION

Birds have not always looked like they do today. They evolved from small reptiles that existed towards the end of the Mesozoic Age, about 200 million years ago. Gradually, perhaps to reach food or shelter, these animals began to walk on their hind legs. As well, perhaps also because of a change in their food and environment, their jaws lengthened and their scales evolved into feathers which helped their bodies to conserve heat. These strange prehistoric birds had horny beaks which looked rather like those of modern birds, but they still had their reptilian teeth. Their wings also showed evidence of their ancestry, retaining three long clawed fingers which helped them to climb trees. Tail feathers, or rectrices, grew in two rows from their long reptilian tails. These 'birds' could not fly, however. Their wings and tails served only as parachutes when jumping from heights or when gliding short distances from one tree to another. A very fine imprint of a pigeon-sized Archaeopteryx, the first known bird, was found in sedimentary limestone excavated near Solnhofen in Bavaria. Their long bones became hollow and filled with air over the course of millions of years and nine air bags, connected with the lungs, developed in the bird's belly. Feathers gradually developed into different types, that is, down and primary coverts. Later, retrices developed and the number of tail vertebrae diminished. Birds began to fly. Only the running birds, or ratites, and swimming birds did not fly because they had adapted themselves too well to their environments. By the Tertiary Age, feathered vertebrate animals similar to present day birds were already living on dry land, in water, and had taken to the air.

All birds devote much time to keeping their feathers in good condition. They are constantly cleaning, preening, and rearranging them. Each long or short feather has to be neatly ordered and in place. This is one reason why they do not like to be touched or stroked. Most water birds condition their feathers with oil from glands on their tails. If water were to reach their bodies, they would lose heat and eventually die from the cold. Parrots and pigeons do not bath and oil themselves as some birds do. Instead the little feathers which grow on their breasts disintegrate into a powder, which keeps their other feathers conditioned. In general, birds' feathers are renewed once or twice a year through moulting. That is why they often have what is called 'nuptial' plumage during mating. The word 'nuptial' means to do with weddings or mating. Male birds usually have bright plumage to attract the attention of females. The females are usually quite dull and ordinary looking, so that they will not be seen easily by other animals who may want to steal their eggs or chicks.

Birds which sleep perched on branches at night do not just have a good sense of balance. On the tendons which bend their toes are special ridges which, under the bird's weight, click into the hollows of the tendon sheaths when the legs bend. When the bird grips the branch, its toes 'lock' themselves and prevent the bird from falling off, even when it is asleep.

Birds' eyes are among the most highly developed in the animal world. They are able to make out even the smallest details. There is an additional third eyelid which is transparent. This is called the 'supercilium'. It protects the eye during flight, under water, and when the light is too bright.

Birds' food varies from small seeds to raw flesh. Some birds may inhabit a rather small territory all year round, whereas other birds may move from area to area in search of food. Those birds which feed mainly on airborne insects migrate in autumn to warmer regions. In spring they return to their old nesting and breeding grounds. During migration they follow the sun, the stars and the Earth's magnetic field. There is also believed to be another factor contributing to their migration, which scientists have yet to discover.

All animals, except man, when left to their own devices will find their place in nature and there will be a balance. They each have their special part to play, and birds are not different.

From earliest times man has captured birds and collected their eggs. Later, he domesticated some birds and kept them for food, eggs, feathers, or even sport, such as cock fighting or hunting. Birds of prey and owls occasionally snatched a chicken or a hen, and were, at one time, considered by man to be an enemy. However, as birds of prey were killed, the rodent population grew, causing far greater damage. Man tried to solve the rodent problem by poisoning them, and in so doing, he poisoned the birds which fed on them. Finally, he came to the realization that the only solution to the problem was to protect the carnivorous birds which he had until then been trying to destroy. Birds of prey and owls are protected nowadays and as there are not many old hollow trees, people build nesting boxes for them. Birds have their own jobs to perform in nature. They spread plant seeds, especially berries, they catch great numbers of insects, they pollinate flowers, they feed on predatory fish, and they kill many rodents. No animal, on its own, is harmful or unnecessary. We should all make it our business to know the inhabitants of our precious planet and protect them.

WHAT A BIRD LOOKS LIKE

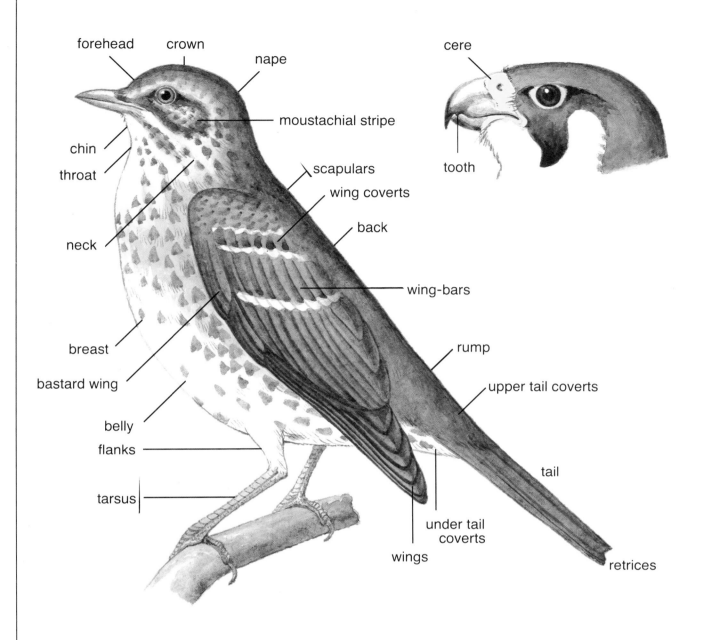

As well as stiff wing coverts and retrices, birds have softer feathers which preserve heat efficiently. These are contour feathers, semiplume, down, sometimes also bristle feathers, bristle/eyelash feathers, and filoplume always found next to contour feathers.

WHAT THE SHAPE OF THE BILL TELLS US

The shape of the bill gives us an idea of what a bird feeds upon.

The Hummingbird extracts the sweet
nectar of flowers.

The Greylag Goose pinches
grass with its bill.

The Goldfinch lives by
gathering seeds.

The Crossbill forces open
cone scales with its crossed
bill and feeds on pine seeds.

The Hawfinch has such
a strong bill that it can
even crack a cherry stone.

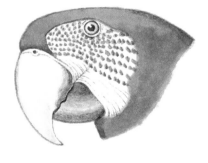

The Parrot cracks seeds and pinches fruit.

The Bullfinch pecks seeds and berries.

The Toucan feeds on juicy sweet fruit.

The Swallow catches insects in flight.

The Avocet feeds on insects and crustaceans in shallow water.

The Woodcock searches for worms and insects by probing in the mud.

The Great Spotted Woodpecker drills holes into tree bark to reach wood insects. It also likes to feed on pine seeds, nuts and acorns.

The Pheasant collects insects, seeds and berries.

The Rook is both herbivorous and carnivorous, occasionally killing rodents.

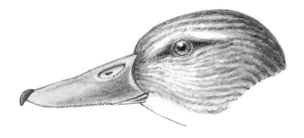

The Mallard filters small shellfish from thin mud.

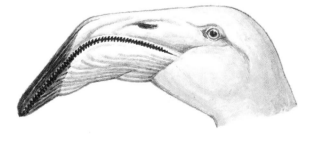

The Flamingo catches crustaceans in a similar way.

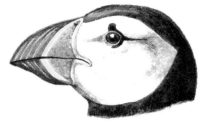

The Puffin catches fish.

The Cormorant is one of the best fish catchers.

The Heron catches not only fish and other water creatures but also feeds on mice and voles.

The Goshawk and the Tawny Owl tear their prey into small pieces.

The Red-backed Shrike catches insects and other small birds.

The Vulture has a bill designed to pick at carcasses.

WHAT THE TAIL DOES

The bird's tail serves as a rudder and a steering surface in flight; as a brake when landing, and as a balance after landing. When a bird lifts its tail up and spreads the feathers or points its tail downwards at the same time dropping its wings and puffing up its feathers, this should be taken as a warning or a threat. White retrices and various coloured spots help the birds to identify each other and stay together when migrating. When a male bird spreads its tail in a fan and ruffles it, this means it is performing a ritual mating dance and is courting a female.

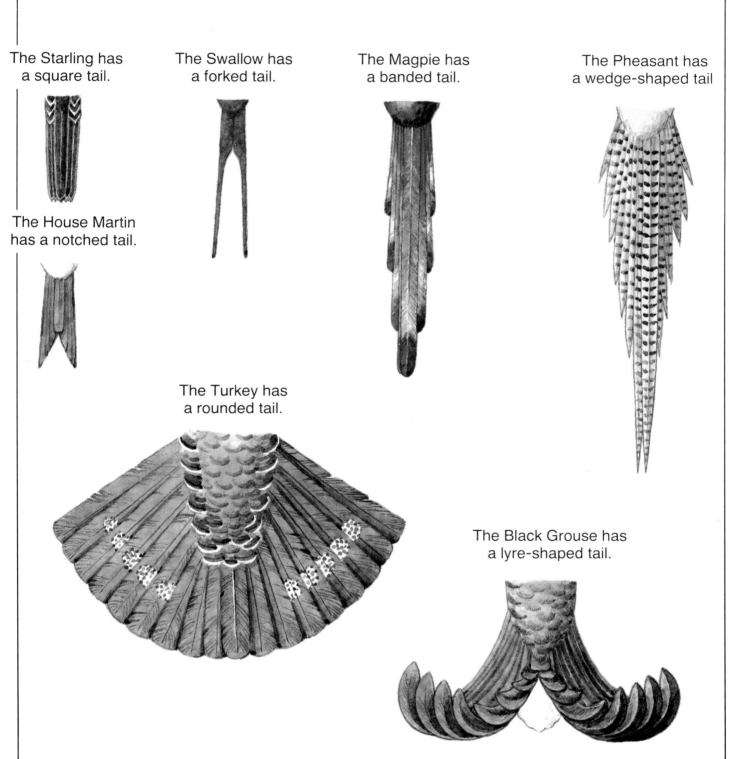

The Starling has a square tail.

The Swallow has a forked tail.

The Magpie has a banded tail.

The Pheasant has a wedge-shaped tail

The House Martin has a notched tail.

The Turkey has a rounded tail.

The Black Grouse has a lyre-shaped tail.

HOW A BIRD FLIES

The most common method of flight is by the flapping of the wings, i.e. 'paddling' or 'rowing' manner.

The Swan 'rows' its wings effortlessly and evenly, with noisy wing beats.

The Eagle-owl also 'rows' but without any noise. We can only sense the whirl of its wings close by because of its soft feathers.

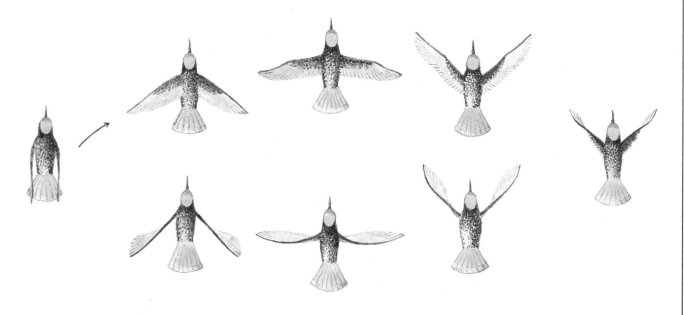

The Hummingbird moves in whirling flight while its body is nearly vertical. It flaps its wings very rapidly — 200 times per second. It hovers in the air and extracts nectar from flowers.

The Kestrel can also hover in one place before
it makes an aerial dive to catch its prey.

The Eagle glides perfectly using its broad
wings, which are rounded at the edges.
Air currents created by warm air allow the
eagle to glide high in the air without ever
flapping its wings.

The Herring Gull has long, narrow, pointed
wings. It also glides. The Gull makes use
of warm layers of air, which move in
different directions above the sea, by gliding
from one layer to another.

WHAT THE SHAPE OF THE LEGS TELLS US

The shape of birds' legs depends on the environment and their method of feeding.

The Blackbird perches easily on branches or walks on the ground.

The Crested Lark keeps its balance on lumps of soil using its long spur.

The Great Bustard is a good runner because it has fewer toes.

The Pheasant rummages for insects.

The Cuckoo can turn its outer forward toe backwards. It is said to have an 'opposable' toe.

The Parrot uses its 'opposable' toe to climb smooth branches.

The Tawny Owl can also turn its outer forward toe backwards in order to get a better grip on a captive mouse.

The Sparrowhawk grips and pierces its prey with its long sharp sickle-like talons.

The Osprey has rough scales on the underside of its toes so that a captured fish cannot slip out.

The Woodpecker has a so-called climbing foot because its inner forward toe is permanently back to front.

The Nightjar has short and weak legs making it unable to walk.

The Swift only uses its legs for short rest periods on walls.

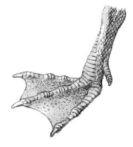

The Duck swims very well.
It can dive. It does not
sink into the mud.

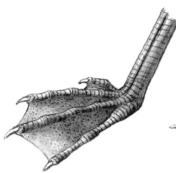

The Cormorant is a good
swimmer and it can also
perch on a branch.

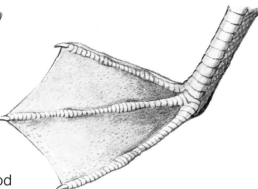

The Albatross can also
rummage in the water with
its oar-like feet.

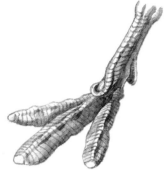

The Grebe spends all its
time in water.

The Coot can swim
or walk in marshland.

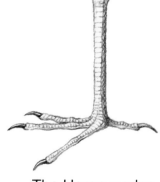

The Heron wades.
The long toes distribute its
weight so that it does not
sink into the mud.

The Moorhen also runs
across the floating foliage
of water plants.

The Flamingo is a wader,
too. It does not sink into
the soft mud because it
has webs between its toes.

A bird's legs may be either bare or fledged.

The Ibis has bare legs.

The Kestrel has 'flanks'
down to its feet.

The Barn Owl has both
fledged tarsi and toes.

THE CLASSIFICATION OF BIRDS

Birds can be divided into running birds or 'ratites', swimming birds or 'swimmers',
and flying birds or 'fliers'.

RATITES

Ratites have underdeveloped wings but well developed legs. Some of them run faster than
racing horses. They live in great savannahs, pampas and steppes. They feed on seeds
and insects. The females lay eggs in the nest, which is usually a shallow hole.
Later on, the male will look after the young.

The **Ostrich** was already kept in ancient
Rome where ostrich races were held. Later,
when ostrich feathers became fashionable
in Europe, many of these fine birds were
killed just to satisfy human vanity.

The South American **Greater Rhea**
and the Australian **Emu** have adapted
well to a European climate and breed
in captivity. They are kept in zoos
and game reserves.

SWIMMERS

These birds are adapted to life in the water. They cannot fly because their wings serve as
oars. Their short, thick feathers resemble rough hair. They have among them the best divers
of the bird world — the Emperor Penguin. They live in the Antarctic. The female lays one
egg, keeping it on her legs and covering it with a belly fold so that it does not become
chilled. She must stand still and cannot move at this time. She starves for a week or longer
before the male takes his turn keeping the egg warm.

The **Emperor Penguin** is the biggest and
most attractively coloured of all penguins.
It can be up to 120 cm tall. The **Jackass
Penguin** is smaller. The **King Penguin**
inhabits the southern tip of South America.
We can only see penguins in the large zoos.
They are rather difficult to keep as they
require a cold climate, icy water, sometimes
sea water, and a daily supply of fresh
sea fish.

FLIERS

There are between 28 and 30 orders of flying birds in the world. There are 20 different orders of birds which live in Europe or are known to us from zoos, and these can be divided into the following categories.

DIVERS

GULLS, TERNS AND RELATIVES

TUBENOSES

PIGEONS AND DOVES

PELICANS AND RELATIVES

PARROTS

STORKS AND HERONS

CUCKOOS

FLAMINGOS

OWLS

WATERFOWL AND SAWBILLS

NIGHTJARS

BIRDS OF PREY

SWIFTS

GAMEBIRDS

KINGFISHERS, ROLLERS, HOOPOES AND RELATIVES

RAILS, CRANES AND RELATIVES

WOODPECKERS AND RELATIVES

WADERS

SONGBIRDS

WELL-KNOWN FLYING BIRDS

DIVERS

Divers have rounded bodies, slim necks and very short tails. The legs form perfect oars and are situated so far back that these birds cannot take off from the ground. They spend their entire lives on water. They build floating nests from aquatic plants and stalks among reeds. The young are small, light and cannot dive. The female Diver forms pockets between her body and wings in which she carries her young. Before diving she closes the pockets and goes under water with her young. The divers feed on water insects and small predatory fish.

Summer

Winter

The **Black-throated Diver** appears in Central and Southern Europe in autumn; if the winter is harsh even earlier — in spring.

The **Little Grebe** is the smallest and the most common of the grebes. It also lives on the smallest overgrown ponds.

The **Great Crested Grebe** has its feathers arranged in a kind of a collar with a double crest on its crown.

TUBENOSES

The nostrils of these birds are extended into special little tubes. They can be seen flying for hours above the waters of seas and oceans without ever flapping their wings. They usually cannot dive and pick up fish and other sea creatures from the surface. One group is called Storm Petrels because they hunt for food when the winds are strong. They snatch their prey from the ridges of waves.

The **Storm Petrel**, the smallest European seabird, is occasionally driven on to the mainland by gales.

The **Fulmar** resembles the Common Gull in its appearance and markings. Its nesting grounds are to be found around the coasts of Scandinavia and Britain and in the Arctic region.

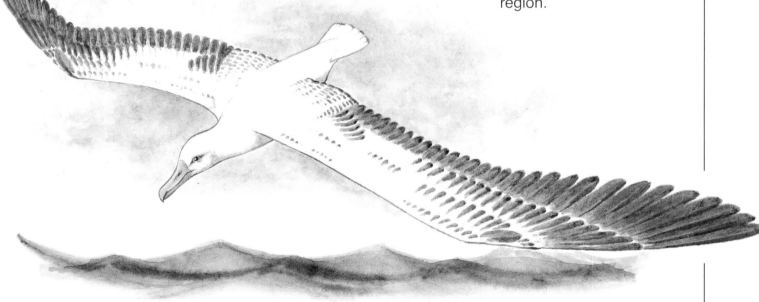

The **Wandering Albatross** is the largest seabird among the Tubenoses, with a wingspan of over 3 metres. It is by far the best flier. Once a year, albatrosses make a long journey to an island in the Pacific where they have had their dug-out nest burrows for centuries. They feed their young the equivalent of twice their own adult body weight before leaving them and setting off on their return journey. The young live on this stored food and only set off to join their parents when they are fully feathered.

PELICANS AND RELATIVES

These birds have long necks, hooked bills, and a membraneous pouch under the lower jaw. All four toes are turned forward and connected by webs. They are excellent fish-catching birds.

The **Eastern White Pelican** and the **Dalmatian Pelican** are found only in Europe in the Danube Delta. They cannot dive and hunt together by forming a line and forcing fish to the shallow waters near the river edge.

The **Cormorant** is found on sea coasts and large river estuaries. It nests in large colonies on trees of small isles and slopes of rocks or cliffs.

STORKS AND HERONS

These are also water birds. They have long legs, long necks and straight, thick bills. They catch fish and amphibians or rodents in marshy meadows and fields.

The **Black-crowned Night Heron** lives in wetland forests and bushy swamps, especially in the Mediterranean.

The **Grey Heron** lurks motionless in reeds and with its dagger-like beak swoops in a split second at its prey. It nests in tree colonies, called heronries. It winters in the south of Europe and in northern Africa. However, many birds remain close to their nesting grounds.

The **White Stork** does not make any sound, it claps its bill and while nesting it may hiss. The young White Stork has black legs and a black beak, whereas in the adults they are red.

The **Black Stork** is slightly smaller. It prefers quiet places. It can be found in large forests where it can find plenty of food. It is also found in wetlands and near streams.

The **Glossy Ibis** nests in colonies mainly in Southern Europe or Asia, usually in heronries.

The **Spoonbill** inhabits river estuaries and swamps in large colonies. It probes for insects, crustaceans, molluscs and even vegetable matter in shallow waters.

FLAMINGOS

These birds have long necks and legs and webbed feet. They nest in colonies by shallow waters, lakesides and river estuaries in warmer climates.

The **Greater Flamingo** can also be found in Southern Europe.
Its bright plumage depends on the colour of its food and,
therefore, in some zoos it becomes virtually white.

WATERFOWL AND SAWBILLS

These birds can swim easily and are good flyers as well. They have short legs with the three forward toes connected by webs. The edges of their flat bills are equipped with transverse knobs topped with sensatory nails. They take in water through a half-opened bill and filter it through these knobs. The worms and larvae of water insects remain on their tongues. They also feed on grass, roots and small fish.

Greylag Geese live in pairs. They regularly return to their nesting grounds, and migrate to northern Africa in winter.

The **Mute Swan** was, in the past, kept on country estates for purely decorative reasons. At present it also nests on small ponds. When threatened, the male Mute Swan fiercely defends its floating nest and its young. In recent years the Mute Swan has become widespread throughout Europe.

The **Mallard** usually nests by a pond, but occasionally further from water, for example in a hollow tree in a wood. The newly hatched young are agile. They can follow their mother and jump down from a great height. No harm comes to them in doing this, as they are very light. Mallards are water birds but they can often be seen searching for food in fields at dusk.

The **Pintail** has a slim neck and conspicuously long tail feathers. It is common especially in Scandinavia and in northern parts of Russia.

The **Shoveler** prefers marshes and reed-fringed lagoons. It nests on wetlands.

The **Goldeneye**, or Northern Duck, nests on the mainland, on riverbanks, by lakes, in the holes in trees, or in suspended nesting boxes.

The **Goosander** can make its nest in a ground cavity if there are not enough tree holes. The female Goosander is the only member of the duck family which carries its young on its back.

BIRDS OF PREY

Easily recognized by their sharp hooked bill and long sickle-like claws, they hunt smaller quadrupeds and birds. They tear their prey into smaller bits and devour them. If the birds only ate flesh, they would lack the essential materials for life. They throw up the undigested remains of bones, hairs and feathers in the shape of cylindrical tufts. These are called pellets. Their eyesight is by far the best of all birds.

The **Honey Buzzard** mostly feeds on larvae and adult wasps and bees whose honeycombs it unearths from the ground with its blunt talons. It winters in tropical Africa.

The **Red Kite** inhabits downland woods. It usually decorates its nest with paper, cloth and other found objects. In winter it migrates from its northern breeding grounds to the Mediterranean.

The **White-tailed Eagle**, the largest European bird of prey, hunts for fish, but also feeds on carcasses.

The **Griffon Vulture** feeds on carrion. It inhabits the huge mountain ridges in the south.

The **Egyptian Vulture** nests in the south, in cliffs or in trees. It often moves close to towns to scavenge on human waste and rubbish.

The **Marsh Harrier** flies at ground level above marshland and overgrown reed ponds. It feeds on small vertebrates.

The **Montagu's Harrier** flies low above marshes and meadows. Its flight is rather slow and laboured. It makes its nest on the ground, in meadows or cornfields, preferably close to water.

The **Goshawk** prefers coniferous forests. It preys on animals up to the size of rabbits. It nests high in trees, with its nest close to the tree trunk.

The **Sparrowhawk** inhabits thinly wooded areas. It swoops on small birds in flight or on the ground. Its short wings and long fanned tail allow for highly agile flight when navigating and avoiding obstacles.

The **Buzzard** hovers low over fields and when it spots its prey, makes a headlong dive. It can also lie patiently in wait close to a burrow. It prefers countryside with both open and wooded areas.

The **Lesser Spotted Eagle** prefers woodland margins with a good view of open areas. It nests in high trees, often close to water. It migrates to eastern Africa in winter.

The **Golden Eagle** is not fully grown until it is three years old. This is relatively late. It preys on marmots, pouched marmots and other rodents but it may also scavenge on carrion.

The **Osprey** hunts only fish. It captures them in a headlong dive to the water's surface. It migrates to tropical and southern Africa in winter.

The **Kestrel** inhabits forests and towns as well. It nests in trees and in blocks of flats. It feeds mainly on mice, voles and larger insects. In towns it frequently hunts sparrows.

The **Hobby** prefers regions with open and wooded areas. It chases and captures small birds and large flying insects in flight. It uses abandoned nests of crows and pigeons for breeding. It winters in eastern and southern Africa.

The **Saker**, a central Asian bird of prey, inhabits wide steppes and wildernesses. It also appears in south-east Europe. In the past, it was kept and trained to hunt, as was the Peregrine.

The **Peregrine** has declined markedly in Europe. It nests in cliffs, ruins or in old tree nests. Its favourite prey is pigeon, which it catches in flight.

GAMEBIRDS

Gamebirds fly clumsily and noisily over short distances only, as their wings are short. They rummage for insects and larvae using their feet which have wide and blunt talons. They also collect seeds and berries. They nest in hollows on the ground but some species roost in trees at night.

The **Black Grouse** prefers moors and peat bogs where ritual male courtship dances take place at dawn.

The **Capercaillie** is a large, less agile bird. It prefers thick mountain forests and seclusion.

The **Grey Partridge** was common in the past. The development of large agricultural fields, together with the use of chemical fertilizers and pesticides on fields and meadows have led to its decline and even disappearance in some areas.

The **Pheasant** originated in Asia. It lives in woods and fields. It is also bred in captivity, in hatcheries.

Other species which belong to gamebirds are the
Domestic Fowl, which comes from Asia, the **Common Turkey**
from North America, the **Common Peafowl**, native of India, and
the **Helmeted Guineafowl** from Africa.

RAILS, CRANES AND RELATIVES

These birds are residents of freshwater marshes, reed beds and fields. They eat both animal and vegetable matter.

The **Water Rail** has a very narrow body for easy movement through dense rushes and reeds. Its calls sound like the squeals of a pig. It migrates to the Mediterranean in winter; some birds visit the British Isles.

The **Moorhen** inhabits small ponds too. It takes off laboriously and needs a long stretch of water. Some birds live all year by ice-free waters, others migrate south or to the west for the winter.

The **Coot** appears in large flocks on open fresh water once the breeding season is over. It is easily distinguished by its white frontal sheet and the characteristic rocking movements of its neck.

The **Common Crane** is found in swampy forests and marshes in north-east Europe, and, more recently, in Central Europe. During courtship, groups of cranes meet at traditional display grounds for dancing ceremonies before sunrise. In the course of this interesting show, the birds hop, bow and spread their wings. The nest is built on the ground in marshes or reed beds. In autumn they migrate high in the sky, often at night, and from time to time they can be heard trumpeting loudly. Their winter quarters are located in the Mediterranean region and in Africa.

The **Great Bustard** is a large bird with long strong legs, and no hind toe. It is found in small flocks in wide plains.

WADERS

Avocets and plovers are strong fliers. They reside close to fresh water and on wetlands. Individual species differ significantly in appearance.

The **Avocet** is seen mostly in shallow muddy waters and river estuaries in south-east Europe and Asia. It nests in colonies close to the water.

The **Little Ringed Plover** is slightly bigger than the Sparrow and hops with quick movements on sandy banks. It winters in the Mediterranean and in Africa.

The **Lapwing** flies in an unusual zig-zag flight on its spring passage. It spends winter in the west of Europe and in Africa.

The **Ruff** resides in Northern Europe and in Asia. When migrating in spring and in autumn it prefers marshlands. The male Ruff boasts an elaborate collar of plumage in spring. During passage the males fight for females.

The **Woodcock** inhabits damp mixed woods. Its long, perceptive beak is used to probe for worms and larvae in soft soil. In spring, shortly after sunset, the males slowly fly low over woodland clearings. Its nest is usually built at the foot of a tree.

The **Curlew** is the largest European wader and occurs in marshes and wet meadows. It winters in the Mediterranean region and in Africa.

GULLS, TERNS AND RELATIVES

These are water birds with long narrow wings which cross over when folded. They are among the best fliers. They have short legs with webbed feet. Many of them live and nest in colonies.

The **Arctic Skua** acquires its food in an unusual way. It chases a single gull until the gull regurgitates its catch. For this reason, gulls will often attack an Arctic Skua, making loud noises, if they spot one nearby.

The **Black-headed Gull** searches for food — worms, slugs, insects and mice — in fields, sometimes at a distance from water.

The **Common Tern** nests on small islets in areas dotted with lakes. It migrates to the coast of southern Africa in winter.

The **Black Tern**, resident in temperate climates, builds its floating nest on a mound of vegetation.

The **Razorbill** lives close to the shore in the North, namely on rock ledges, in large colonies.

The **Puffin** is easily recognized by its multicoloured bill. It dives to catch small fish under water. It nests in burrows dug on small grassy islets.

PIGEONS AND DOVES

These birds have soft bills which are swollen at the root. They live in permanent pairs. They feed on vegetable matter.

The **Pigeon** which lives in cities is a descendant of the Rock Dove. It has become a nuisance to man. Its droppings dirty and damage historical monuments and buildings.

The **Woodpigeon** occurs in all types of woods and forests. It has recently appeared in city parks as well. It can be recognized by its white neck slashes.

The **Collared Dove**, a native of Asia Minor, has become very common in recent years. It feeds on seeds and various left-overs.

The **Turtle Dove** builds its nest in the cover of thin, mixed woods. It migrates in winter, especially to Africa.

PARROTS

Parrots usually have brilliant plumage. They have an 'opposable' toe and a strong hooked bill. They live in permanent pairs and make their nests in tree hollows. They are popular in zoos because of their appearance and their ability to imitate the human voice. The parrot family includes about 340 species. They are natives of southern Asia, Africa, America and Australia.

The Grey Parrot
Africa

The Masked Lovebird
Africa

The Yendaya Conure
South America

The Crimson Rosella
Australia

The Plum-head Parrakeet
Asia

CUCKOOS

Living in the tropics and subtropical regions, cuckoos have a deeply cleft bill, a banded tail and an 'opposable' toe.

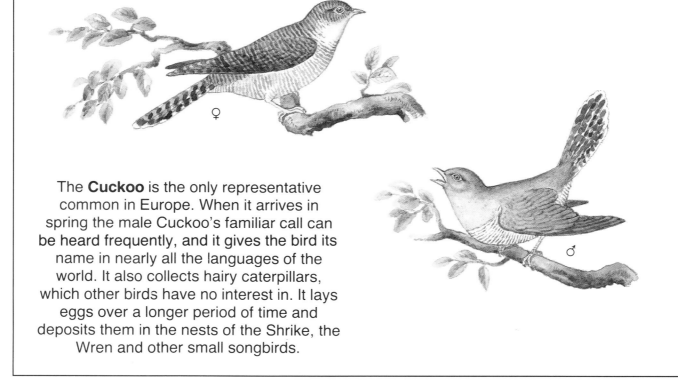

The **Cuckoo** is the only representative common in Europe. When it arrives in spring the male Cuckoo's familiar call can be heard frequently, and it gives the bird its name in nearly all the languages of the world. It also collects hairy caterpillars, which other birds have no interest in. It lays eggs over a longer period of time and deposits them in the nests of the Shrike, the Wren and other small songbirds.

OWLS

Owls have short, rounded bodies covered with soft plumage enabling them to fly silently. Their hooked sharp bills and long sickle-like talons are well hidden in their feathers. Their large eyes are directed forwards, close to each other, with small feathers arranged in a facial 'disk'. These nocturnal birds can also see during daylight, although only in black and white. They usually feed on mice and insects and are, for this reason, considered very beneficial to man. They regurgitate the undigested remains in the form of grey cylindrical pellets, similar to the birds of prey. In spring, when mating they make low 'oo-oo-oo' calls.

The **Barn Owl** inhabits church towers and barn lofts. It occurs in two forms — the white-breasted and the rare dark-breasted.

The **Eagle-owl**, the largest European owl, is quite rare. It resides in wooded rocks but hunts for food in open areas. It captures prey up to the size of rabbits.

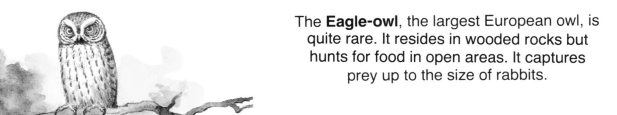

The **Eurasian Pygmy Owl**, the smallest of the European owls, is agile in daylight as well. It hunts voles and also attacks small birds in flight. It uses the old holes of the Great Spotted Woodpecker. It is found in mountainous forests and in woods at the foot of mountains.

The **Little Owl** resides close to human habitation. It is a small bird which finds sufficient nourishment in insects and earthworms. It nests in holes in trees or buildings, or in barn lofts. Sometimes, attracted by light, it comes to perch on window sills. It hoots and shrieks, which can be terrifying in the stillness of the night.

The **Tawny Owl** occurs in two forms — the brown and the grey. It resides both in woods and town parks.

The **Long-eared Owl** resembles the Eagle-owl but it is much smaller and slimmer. It inhabits hedgerows and uses the abandoned nests of crows and squirrels. In winters with heavy snowfall it suffers greatly from lack of food.

The **Short-eared Owl** prefers freshwater marshes, moors, wet meadows or sandy dunes. It usually flies low, hunting in the early dusk, but often during daylight. If voles become very numerous, it hunts in the company of others (in parliaments of owls).

40

NIGHTJARS

These nocturnal, insectivorous birds are from the tropics. They have wide flat heads with large eyes, and deeply cleft beaks surrounded by long sensory feathers.

The **Nightjar** is the only representative of this order in Europe.
It likes to fly close to grazing cattle, catching large hawk-moths
and noctuid moths.

SWIFTS

These birds spend most of their lives held airborne by their wings. They feed in flight, they collect building material for their nests while flying. Some swifts even sleep while on the wing, high in the air. Hummingbirds inhabit American tropical and subtropical forests and even areas spreading to Alaska. Some birds are very small in size, similar to the Bumble Bee.

The **Swift** can reach speeds of up to 220 km per hour. It has underdeveloped legs, with all four toes reversed to the front so that it is unable to walk. It nests in rocks and on tall buildings, and makes high-pitched screams while flying. It remains in its European breeding grounds for only three months and then migrates to southern Africa.

The **Sparkling Violetear** lives in the area from Bolivia to Colombia. It feeds on nectar and small insects.

KINGFISHERS, ROLLERS, HOOPOES AND RELATIVES

These are brightly coloured birds which have partially joined toes. Their beaks are usually deeply cloven.

The **Kingfisher** is only found near streams and rivers. It feeds on small fish and water insects. For this reason it often goes hungry in winter.

The **European Bee-eater** lives communally, preferably near water. It nests in burrows dug in clay embankments and sand quarries. It often perches on telephone lines and lies in wait for flying insects, especially wasps and bees. It favours a warm climate and resides in Southern Europe, in Asia Minor and northern Africa.

The **European Roller** favours lowland woods with abundant hollow trees. It migrates to eastern Africa in winter.

The **Hoopoe** lives mostly in pastures and meadows in open country where there are trees with holes. The hole with the nestlings is foul smelling because of excrement and liquid from the cloaca, which the nestlings are able to eject at intruders. The Hoopoe migrates to Africa for the winter.

WOODPECKERS AND RELATIVES

These birds have straight strong bills, usually wedge-shaped, and long flexible tongues. Their special feet and strong legs enable them to creep up tree trunks; their tail feathers are stiff.

The **Wryneck** nests in rotting trees in gardens and orchards. It does not climb trees. When a predator approaches, it straightens its neck and twists its head, making loud hissing sounds. The snake-like hissing usually scares off its attacker. It winters in Africa.

The **Green Woodpecker** lives in deciduous woods, tree avenues or orchards. It likes to rummage in ant hills. It prefers to feed on ants, wood-eating insects, beech mast and acorns.

The **Black Woodpecker** likes extensive woods. It nests in holes in trees and feeds on insects and seeds. It climbs tree trunks and extracts insect larvae living under the bark and in the wood.

The **Great Spotted Woodpecker** is the most common treecreeper. It especially likes pine seeds. It first lodges a pine cone in a tree crevice and then strikes at it with its bill. In autumn it searches for food in gardens.

The **Toco Toucan** has a strikingly large beak, which is, however, quite light in weight. It belongs with the creepers but does not climb trees. Several species of the toucan live in Central and South America.

SONGBIRDS

The birds have a perfectly developed singing apparatus. They mark their territories against birds of the same species by singing. Therefore, they are mostly heard in spring, during the mating period. They feed on seeds, berries and insects. The young usually feed on insects because they include all the essential nutrition for their rapid growth.

The **Crested Lark**, originally a native of the steppes, occurs close to human habitation. It resembles the Skylark but can be distinguished easily by its small helm-like crest.

The **Skylark** flies high in the skies where it flutters and sings its songs. It then draws its wings close to its body and falls to the ground like a stone. Only when it gets close to the ground, does it glide to land. It produces eggs twice a year in a shallow nest on the ground.

The **Sand Martin** lives in large colonies in the steep banks of abandoned sand quarries. It digs a long hole in the sand bank and lines its nest with feathers.

The **Swallow** and the **House Martin** inhabited rocky areas in the past. In time they discovered that they could find their food — flies and mosquitoes — in larger numbers near where people live. The Swallow has a rusty red spot on its forehead and throat, its tail resembles a fork. The House Martin has a bright white rump and the bottom of the body and its tail is less forked. The Swallow builds its nest inside buildings whereas the House Martin makes its nest outside, under the roof, often forming colonies. In recent years the numbers of Swallows and House Martins have declined.

The **Tree Pipit** is a bird of wood margins and hollows. It flies high in its song flight, then flutters back to the same perch. It winters in the Mediterranean and Africa.

The **Grey Wagtail** moves briskly along the stony banks of streams and brooks. It migrates to Southern Europe and northern Africa in winter.

The **White Wagtail** frequently wags its long tail. It is found close to water, in pastures, and near where people live.

The **Waxwing**, an insectivorous inhabitant of the coniferous woods of northern Scandinavia and the northern parts of Russia, is an occasional winter visitor to Central Europe. It often arrives in large flocks and prefers to feed on rowan berries.

The **Dipper** is found by fast-running waters and mountain and hill streams. It is the size of the Blackbird. It can be recognized by its short tail and large white breast. It dives and moves fast under water where it catches the larvae of aquatic insects.

The **Wren** is one of the smallest birds but its call is quite distinctive and loud. It favours mixed woods, banks of streams and overgrown gardens. In addition to building a nest, it also builds various shelters in which it occasionally sleeps or finds refuge.

The **Robin** inhabits woodlands, orchards and gardens. Its pleasant call and thin, sad-sounding song can often be heard in spring and summer.

The **Nightingale** resembles the Robin both in appearance and in size. It is considered to be the most fabulous songster. Its beautiful trills resound after dark but also frequently during the day. It nests in bushes close to the ground in woodlands and overgrown gardens.

The **Black Redstart** inhabits cliffs and also towns and cities. It builds its nest in places such as a rock crevice, an old lantern or under a roof beam. It is continuously on the move, hopping to a different perch and shaking its rusty-red tail with jerky movements.

The **Whinchat** likes fallow land and moors covered with small bushes on which it can perch. It then pounces to the ground to feed on various insects. It winters in the Mediterranean and in northern Africa.

The **Wheatear** makes sudden darting movements. It nests in holes in the ground or in rock crevices in stone or sand quarries or stony fallow lands. It migrates to Africa in winter.

The **Blackbird** has moved from woods closer to where people live. Its merry and cheeky whistling announces the arrival of spring. The woodland variety of the Blackbird remains rather timid and migrates to the south-west in winter. The town Blackbird usually remains resident throughout the year.

The **Fieldfare** forms small colonies along tree avenues, tree groupings and wood margins during the nesting period. It searches for food in nearby meadows. Substantial flocks come to Europe as winter visitors, from as far away as Siberia.

The **Song Thrush** sings loudly and merrily. It carefully lines its deep nesting cup with mud and powdery rotting wood.

The **Grasshopper Warbler** is an invisible inhabitant of overgrown wetlands and marshlands. Its presence can only be detected from its continuous reeling call, which is produced by the male Warbler hidden somewhere under a tuft of grass. It winters as far away as tropical Africa.

The **Reed Warbler** climbs deftly on reed stalks in the dense cover of pond vegetation. It suspends its nest on the reed stalks so firmly that it cannot be dislodged even by the strongest winds. It often becomes a host to the Cuckoo.

The **Icterine Warbler** has an exceptionally strong voice and frequently varies its notes and melodies. It feeds only on insects. It builds a deep nesting cup in gardens, parks and woods, and often decorates it with white birch bark.

The **Whitethroat** flies high in the air in its song flight. It inhabits bushes, brambles and the stems of tall herbs.

The **Blackcap** lives in deciduous woods and makes an untidy, ruffled nesting cup out of dry plants. It searches for juicy berries, especially raspberries and cranberries in autumn.

The **Chiffchaff** inhabits wood margins, hollows, and orchards. Its rounded nesting dome with a side entrance close to the ground is well camouflaged by dry leaves.

The **Goldcrest**, the smallest European bird, makes its home in the tree tops of spruce and deciduous woods. It suspends its nest at the end of an overhanging branch. Some birds are resident throughout the year whereas others migrate to Southern Europe.

The **Spotted Flycatcher** often perches on a raised spot, flying out to catch passing insects. It then returns to its original perch. It is found in wood margins, orchards and near where people live.

The **Pied Flycatcher** restlessly twitches its tail and wings. It does not usually return to its perch after its hunting flight. It nests in tree holes and nest boxes.

The **Bearded Tit** occurs in marshy reed-beds. It wanders occasionally, but tends to remain in the same spot. The males have a typical black moustache.

The **Marsh Tit** nests only once a year, in tree stumps or other holes in rotten wood. It makes its home in parks, gardens and wood margins.

The **Crested Tit** is a permanent resident in spruce and pine woods. It nests twice a year in dug-out holes in old tree stumps.

The **Coal Tit** has a white nape patch and lives in spruce woods in lowlands and highlands.

The **Blue Tit** and the **Great Tit** are very agile. They search every crevice very thoroughly and collect vast numbers of insects and their tiny eggs. They are the most common of all the tits living close to people's homes.

The **Nuthatch** is very agile and can climb up and down trees. If the need arises, it makes the entry to a tree hole smaller, using plastered mud. It inhabits mixed woods and gardens.

The **Wallcreeper** flies in circles around steep mountain slopes like a butterfly, searching for food. It usually winters in the lowlands in old quarries and ruins.

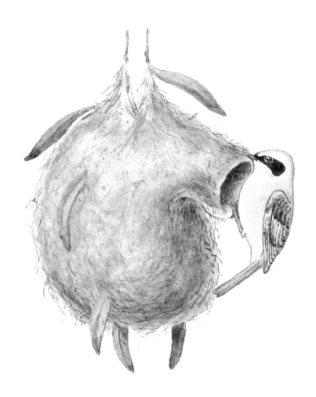

The **Common Treecreeper**, an agile native of coniferous woods, makes its nest under tree bark. In winter it can often be seen in parks climbing up the trees.

The **Penduline Tit** resides close to water in willows and birches. The male makes several nests in spring. It often nests with two or three females. It migrates South in winter.

The **Golden Oriole** favours deciduous woods and groves from which its flute-like whistle can be heard. It migrates to tropical Africa in winter where other similar species are found.

The **Red-backed Shrike** is a songbird which preys on insects and small vertebrates. It stores its prey spiked on the thornbushes of hedgerows. It can imitate the voices of other birds and even the barking of a dog. It migrates to tropical Africa in winter.

The **Great Grey Shrike** often sits on the tops of trees and telegraph poles. It inhabits wood margins, neglected gardens and barren fields surrounded by hedgerows. It only nests once a year and the family unit stays together for a long time.

The **Jay** is a very vigilant bird. It warns others in the wood of any impending danger. It can also imitate various voices — the buzzard's 'kee-kee-keeing', the creaking of a gate, the squeaking of a pump, the cock's 'cock-a-doodle-doo' or the cat's mewing. All species of the raven family are very intelligent and can learn to 'speak' quite easily.

The **Magpie** hunts insects, mice and voles. It also often plunders other birds' nests. It builds its own nest in the crown of a tree or in a blackthorn bush. It is attracted to shiny objects which it keeps in various hiding places.

The **Spotted Nutcracker** is an inhabitant of mountainous conifer forests. It favours pine seeds and hazelnuts, which it hides in the ground. In autumn and in winter, numerous flocks of nutcrackers migrate to Europe from Siberia.

The **Jackdaw** lives in flocks on cliffs, in ruins or towers. Like the Magpie, it is attracted to shiny objects.

The **Hooded Crow** lives mainly in eastern parts of Europe whereas

the **Carrion Crow** is more common in Western Europe. They often interbreed. In spring they plunder the nests of gamebirds. In winter they roam in large numbers.

The **Rook** nests in colonies, called rookeries. In autumn, the resident rooks of Central Europe migrate to the south-west and their place is taken over by the rooks from the Russian plains and even the Urals, which often arrive in numerous flocks.

The **Raven** mainly scavenges on carcasses and refuse. It nests in cliffs and trees. It moves closer to people's homes in winter.

The **Starling** has glossy, metallic nuptial plumage. Its voice is a variety of whistling, wheezing, squeaking and creaking calls. It forms huge flocks outside the breeding season, which can inflict heavy damage on cherry or grape crops. It winters in the Mediterranean or in northern Africa.

The **House Sparrow** can catch enormous numbers of caterpillars and harmful insects during the breeding season. However, it can also cause great damage by feeding on unripened grain, or by nipping out the buds of trees and bushes in winter and in spring.

The **Tree Sparrow** resembles the House Sparrow but it has a white half collar and both sexes have the same plumage. Both species nest twice a year.

The **Chaffinch** is the second most common bird after the Sparrow. Its short merry song can often be heard in spring.

The **Brambling** inhabits the whole of northern Scandinavia and the northern parts of Russia. It is a common winter visitor on the European mainland. It often arrives in very large flocks. It is a very social bird and gets on well with other finch species.

The **Serin** likes to perch on telephone lines, singing its squeaky song persistently. It lives close to people. It builds its nest out of twigs, grass and moss. Large accumulations of excrement in the nest reveal the presence of young, as the Serin, like the Greenfinch and the Goldfinch, does not carry its droppings away.

The **Greenfinch** makes its home in gardens, parks and cemeteries. The bright yellow 'mirrors' on its wings are especially prominent in flight.

The **Goldfinch** prefers open countryside with deciduous trees but it also nests in orchards. It feeds on the seeds of dandelion, thistle, burdock and other weeds. Some birds migrate to the Mediterranean in winter.

The **Siskin** lives in colonies in mountainous conifer forests. In autumn it searches for alder trees and pecks the seeds from their small cones. It usually migrates south in winter, mainly to Italy.

The **Redpoll** is common in Scandinavia, Britain and the mountainous regions of Europe and Asia. Large flocks of northern Redpolls are occasional winter visitors to mainland area.

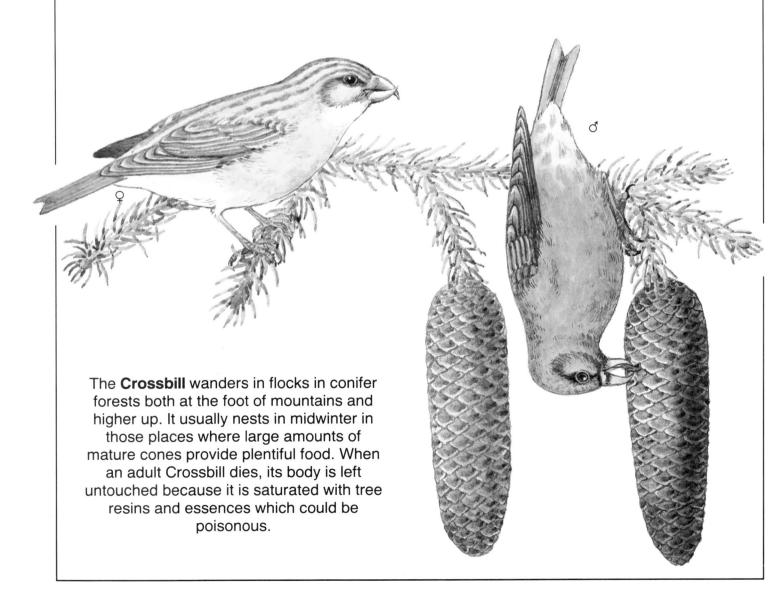

The **Crossbill** wanders in flocks in conifer forests both at the foot of mountains and higher up. It usually nests in midwinter in those places where large amounts of mature cones provide plentiful food. When an adult Crossbill dies, its body is left untouched because it is saturated with tree resins and essences which could be poisonous.

The **Bullfinch** prefers conifer woods but in recent years it has also inhabited parks.

The **Hawfinch** is by far the strongest of all songbirds. It can crack even the toughest seeds with its huge thick bill. It lives in deciduous woods and in gardens.

The **Yellowhammer** was a common field bird in the past. In recent years it has almost disappeared from most of its territories in Europe. It has paid a high price for man's introduction of pesticides as it feeds only on the seeds of weeds.

The **Corn Bunting** is similarly affected by pesticides and shares the Yellowhammer's misfortune. Both species build their nests on the ground, usually twice a year.

WHICH BIRD IS IT?

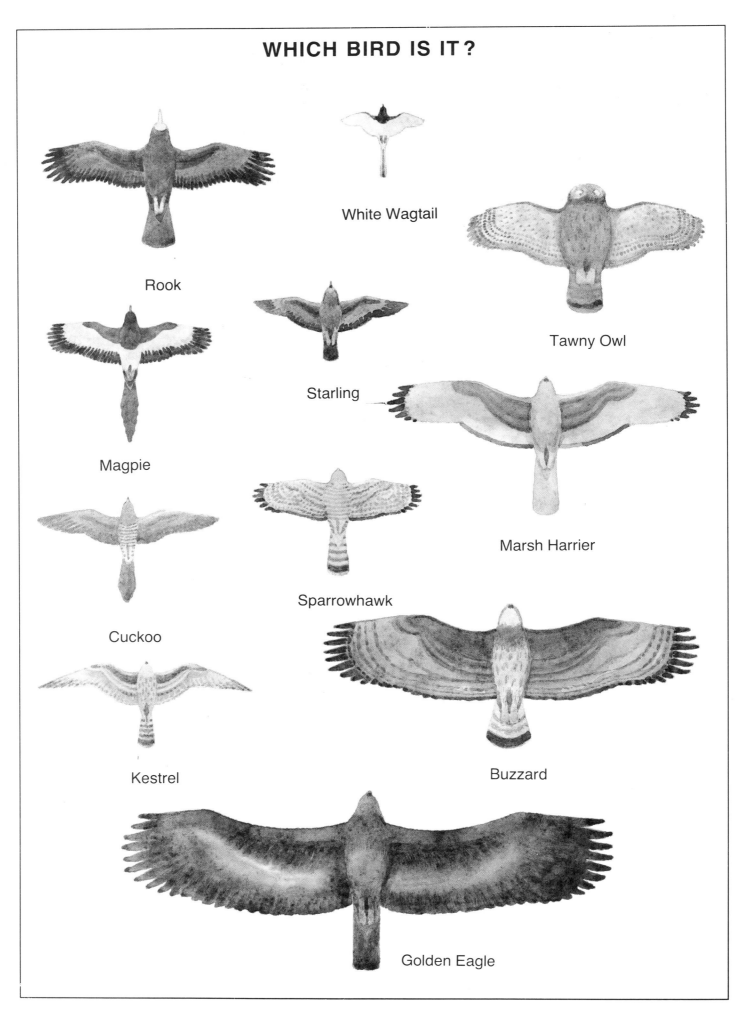

White Wagtail

Rook

Tawny Owl

Starling

Magpie

Marsh Harrier

Sparrowhawk

Cuckoo

Kestrel

Buzzard

Golden Eagle

White Wagtail

Starling

Rook

Cuckoo

Tawny Owl

Sparrowhawk

Crow

Magpie

Kestrel

Golden Eagle

Buzzard

HOW BIRDS DO THEIR COURTING

Spring is the period of courtship. Birds display their nuptial plumage, which is conspicuously brighter and shinier, especially in the males, than their ordinary plumage.

The male Black Grouse first has to fight to establish its territory. In March, males gather on a moorland and hold tournaments. They droop their wings, fan their tails over their backs so that the white feathers on the wings and the white undertail-coverts show. The comb above the eye is a shining bright red. The stronger and the more experienced mature cocks usually win the field.

The Common Peacock shuffles on one spot, struts his body proudly and turns round and round in front of peahens in order to display all his beauty, his dropped wings brushing against the ground and his long tail fanned and lifted again.

The Kingfisher presents his female with a freshly captured fish which it gallantly delivers head first in order that the female may swallow it more easily.

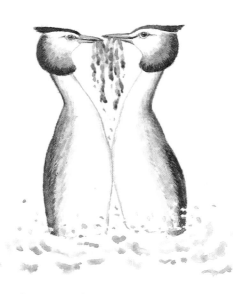

The male Wagtail plays chase with his chosen female during courtship.

The Great Crested Grebe observes a complex courting ritual during which both partners dive and collect aquatic vegetation which they present to each other for use in building a nest.

The Dove is gentle and attentive. The male preens and rearranges the female's feathers and gently caresses her with his bill.

HOW BIRDS BUILD THEIR NESTS

The Pheasant is satisfied with a shallow hole in the ground.

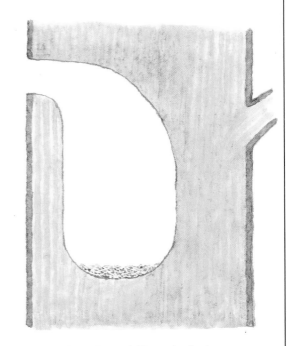

The Black Woodpecker drills a hole in a tree and puts the wood chips at the foot of the nest.

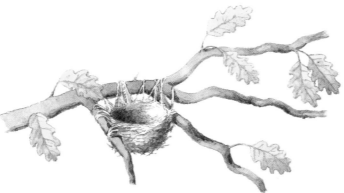

The Golden Oriole forms a cup made of grass, twigs or pieces of string, which is suspended in branches.

The Chaffinch builds a neat cup from grass, moss, lichen and horsehair in low vegetation. It often decorates its cup with white birch bark.

The Kingfisher drills up to a 1 metre deep hole into a steep river bank and lines it with fish bones and scales.

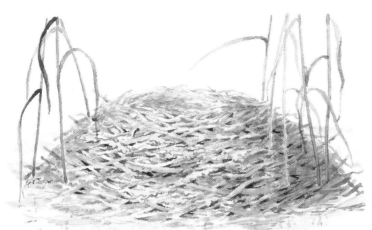

The Great Crested Grebe builds a floating mound in water from the rotting leaves of aquatic vegetation.

The House Martin constructs its hemispherical nest with its tiny entrance, from soft mud. The Swallow attaches its open cup nest with one side to a wall. It only occasionally builds on a firm base.

The Reed Warbler suspends its cup-shaped nest, woven out of plant stems, in reeds.

The Sparrowhawk constructs a large flat nest out of twiglets and twigs, usually in a spruce tree.

The Penduline Tit constructs an ingenious pear-shaped nest with a side entrance, woven from vegetable matter and fibres and situated at the end of a thin tree branch.

The Magpie thoroughly plasters its nest crevice with mud and finally constructs a roof made of thorns.

WHAT A BIRD'S EGG LOOKS LIKE

The Magpie produces oval eggs, which is the most common shape of egg in the bird world.

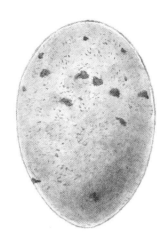

The Great Crested Grebe has elongated eggs, which correspond to its long, slim body.

The Tawny Owl lays rounded eggs in an enclosed tree hole from which they cannot roll away.

The Lapwing lays pear-shaped eggs. The entire clutch can be arranged to form a four-petalled clover leaf shape.

A bird's egg in an open nest, particularly if close to the ground or directly on the ground, has to be camouflaged to protect it from being spotted by an enemy.

Chaffinch

Blackbird

Song Thrush

Crested Lark

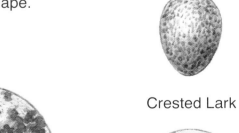

Skylark

Yellowhammer

Black-headed Gull

Common Tern

Little Ringed Plover

Nightjar

HOW MANY EGGS ARE IN THE NEST?

The Eagle usually has only one egg. It could barely support more young even though it hunts over an extensive area.

The Pigeon lays two eggs.

The Lapwing has four eggs, arranged in the nest with tips together, in order that the bird may cover them all with its small body.

The Thrush lays five to six eggs.

The Duck has ten or more eggs.

The Partridge lays at least 15 eggs.

Those species of birds which lose many of their young are forced to lay large numbers of eggs in order that their species does not become extinct.

WHAT IS THE DIFFERENCE BETWEEN ALTRICIAL AND PRECOCIAL BIRDS?

The female patiently incubates the eggs and protects them whatever the weather is like. She leaves the nest only for a short period to find food. The eggs must not become chilled. In some cases both parents share in incubation.

The young which are hatched blind and naked must be fed by their parents. This type of bird is called an altricial bird or feeder.

The Blackbird's young hatch in a fortnight.

They grow quite quickly and, as time goes by, the parents are busier in order to provide food for them.

Finally, the young become so big that they cannot stay in the nest any longer.

Their first flight ends on the ground because they are not yet fully fledged. Their wing and tail feathers are only beginning to grow.

Later on when they can fly quite well and look bigger than their parents, they are still not able to feed on their own and depend on their parents for food.

The Cuckoo is an altricial bird but it neither feeds its young nor builds its own nest. It selects nests belonging to small birds, such as the Wren, and deposits a single egg in each of them.

The newly hatched Cuckoo immediately tries to throw its foster siblings out of the nest. Finally, it succeeds. The Cuckoo, then, has all the food for itself, it grows fast and is even hungrier.

Its foster parents search for food from morning till night, often going hungry themselves. Before it becomes independent, the Cuckoo grows to three times the size of the Wren.

Those birds which are able to see and are clothed in down when they hatch are immediately agile and can feed on their own. They are termed precocial birds or non-feeders.

Pheasant chicks hatch from eggs and as soon as they are dry they are able to run. The hen teaches them how to search for seeds and how to rummage for insects.

The Duck does not feed its ducklings either. It immediately takes them to water to look for food.

WHERE BIRDS MIGRATE TO

When colder autumn days arrive, the majority of our birds migrate to warmer climates where they can find plenty of food. By that time young birds are strong and can fly as well as their parents. The journey to winter habitation is long, sometimes covering a distance of several thousand kilometres. The 'winter guests', birds from the north and north-east, arrive in their place.

The main passage routes are marked in colour on the map, individual species are drawn in their winter habitation.

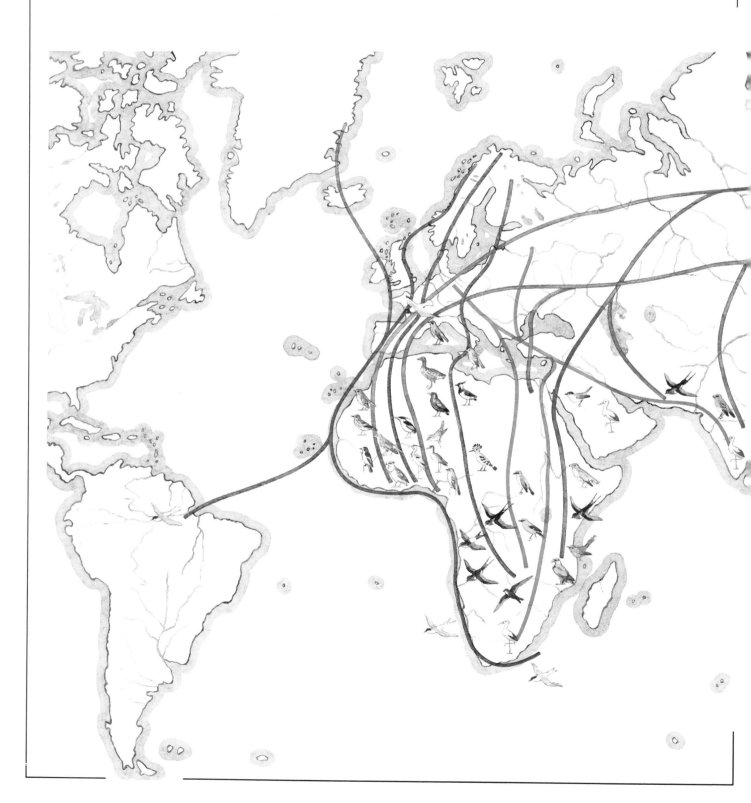

How do we know where and which route birds take? Scientists working at bird-ringing stations, together with volunteer helpers, trap birds in mist-nets and ring them. They also ring the young in nests — they put a light metal band with a number and the address of that station on one leg. When an individual finds a dead bird, he or she removes the ring and sends it to the respective station with details of when, where and under what circumstances the bird was found. At the station, this information is matched with a file stating when and where the original ringing took place, plus the age and sex of the bird. In this manner bird-ringing stations receive information from places as far away as India and southern Africa.

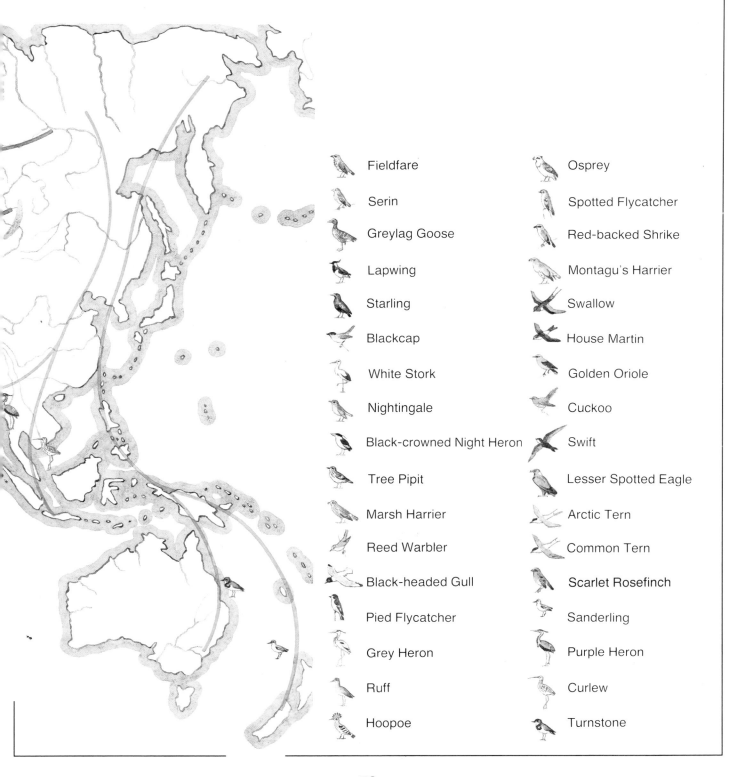

Fieldfare

Serin

Greylag Goose

Lapwing

Starling

Blackcap

White Stork

Nightingale

Black-crowned Night Heron

Tree Pipit

Marsh Harrier

Reed Warbler

Black-headed Gull

Pied Flycatcher

Grey Heron

Ruff

Hoopoe

Osprey

Spotted Flycatcher

Red-backed Shrike

Montagu's Harrier

Swallow

House Martin

Golden Oriole

Cuckoo

Swift

Lesser Spotted Eagle

Arctic Tern

Common Tern

Scarlet Rosefinch

Sanderling

Purple Heron

Curlew

Turnstone

WHO ARE 'WINTER GUESTS'?

Siskin

Bullfinch

Waxwing

Redpoll

Brambling

Spotted Nutcracker

Fieldfare

Rook

Short-eared Owl

WHOSE PRINT IS IT?

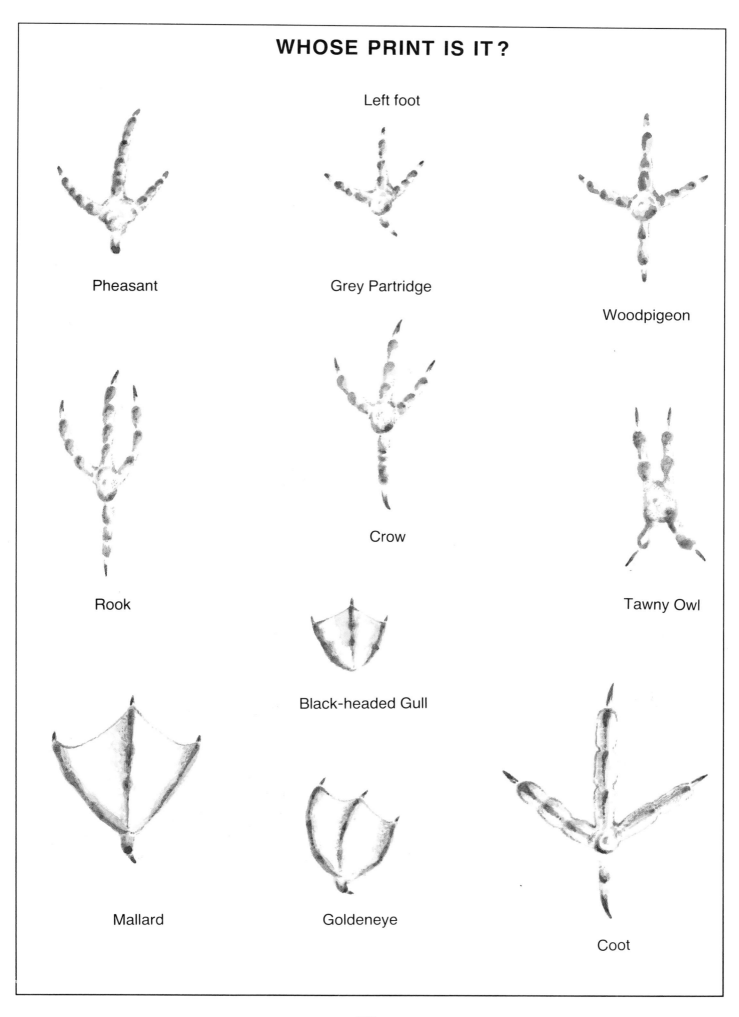

Left foot

Pheasant

Grey Partridge

Woodpigeon

Rook

Crow

Tawny Owl

Black-headed Gull

Mallard

Goldeneye

Coot

WHICH SPECIES OF BIRDS ARE ENDANGERED?

Most bird species are not in danger. Some species which have become rare are called endangered species. The numbers of such species increase each year.

Penduline Tit

Nightjar

Redstart

Red-backed Shrike

Crested Lark

Wryneck

Curlew

Hoopoe

Barn Owl

Black Grouse

Capercaillie

Peregrine

Red Kite

Purple Heron

Saker

White-tailed Eagle

Great Bustard

HOW BIRDS ARE BENEFICIAL TO MAN

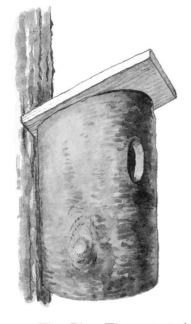

The Blue Tit nests twice a year, the first time in April to May when it lays eight to ten eggs; the second clutch is in June and is smaller, comprising six to eight eggs. Just imagine how many insects this Tit collects if the adult bird consumes as much food as it weighs every day!

The Great Tit is larger than the Blue Tit and lays two or three more eggs as well. It also nests twice a year.

The Kestrel catches fourteen mice or voles daily for its four to six young. When food is plentiful it will breed twice in one year.

The Buzzard will catch, according to research data, around two thousand voles in a year. One vole is estimated to consume about 2 kg of grain in a year. This means that a single Buzzard can save a farmer about 4 tonnes of grain a year.

INDEX

Numbers in bold refer to main entries

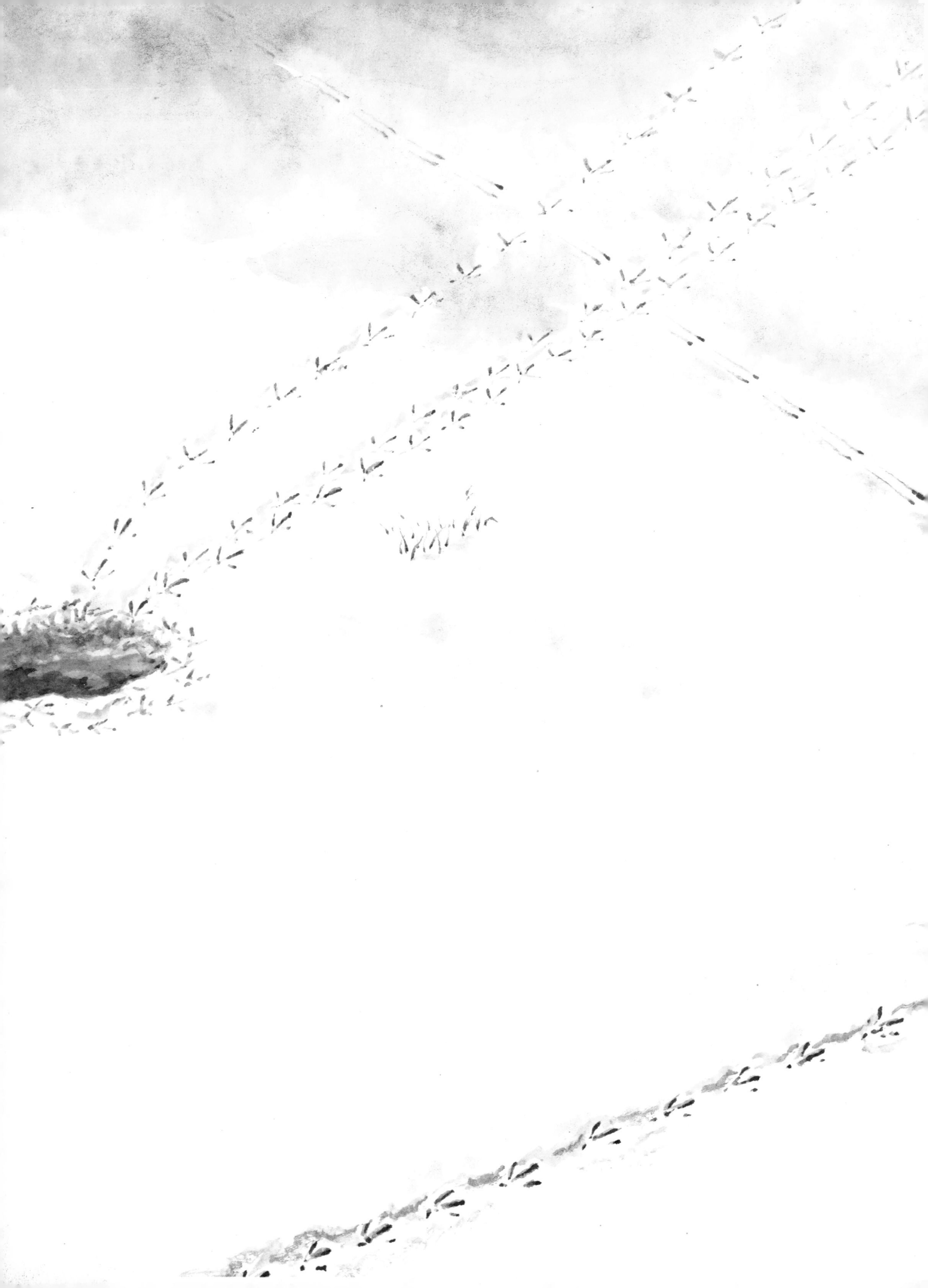